Why Most Lawyers Are INVISIBLE To Affluent Clients

The Attorney Authority
SNOWBALL

BY **RICHARD JACOBS**

Jacobs & Whitehall
73-03 Bell Blvd, #10
Oakland Gardens, NY 11364
www.jacobsandwhitehall.com

Ordering Information:

Quantity sales. Special discounts are available on quantity purchases by corporations, associations, and others. For details, contact the publisher at the address above.

Orders by U.S. trade bookstores and wholesalers. Please contact Jacobs & Whitehall: Tel: (888) 991-2766 or visit www.jacobsandwhitehall.com.

Printed in the United States of America

Published in 2021

ISBN: 978-1-954506-08-4

DISCLAIMER

This publication is intended to be used for educational purposes only. No writer-reader relationship is intended to be created by reading this material. The publisher, authors, and all business associates assume no liability for any errors or omissions or for how this book or its contents are used or interpreted or for any consequences resulting directly or indirectly from the use of this book or the material therein.

If you are an attorney, please know that the material in this book may conflict with local, state or federal bar requirements, ethics requirements for being an attorney, or other requirements or laws. Nothing in this book should be construed to be legal, ethical, or otherwise. Your implementation, reliance on, or use of any of the information contained in this book is at your own risk.

TESTIMONIALS

"I signed up with Speakeasy Marketing in the summer of the pandemic. recognizing a new normal, and practicing family law and divorce mediation for over 30 years, I saw a new opportunity rising. I worked hard creating lots of on line content, and was guided at every step by the wonderful team I hired. it is now four months since I began this new venture, and I am already seeing some positive results. I am confident that the next calendar quarter will continue on the same trajectory. I am very grateful for this crackerjack team; they made it all worthwhile."

— Alan Finkel, Esq.

****

"The plan Speakeasy Marketing put together to ramp up my marketing was phenomenal. Traffic to my website has definitely increased and the staff is responsive to my inquiries. I would highly recommend to anyone seeking to grow a business."

— Lisa Pezzano Mickey, Esq.

****

"Ten years ago I was floundering in my internet marketing. I had experienced a number of companies both large and small who promised the world but never delivered. Then I discovered Speakeasy Marketing. Although there is no limit to the number of leads attorneys desire, I am quite satisfied with my online presence and the continued efforts to improve it. Moreover, their staff is always available for consultation and each atty is assigned an individual representative. This goes a long way in making me feel like I am not just one of many but an individual with individual needs."

— Mike Kramer, Esq.

****

"I've been working with Speakeasy Marketing for over a year now and have been very happy with their overall quality of service. My account manager, Michelle Farrar and the staff was very professional, helpful and responsive to my firm's needs. I would recommend Speakeasy to anyone in need of marketing services."

— Shant Chakerian, Esq.

****

"I have had an amazing experience working with Amber and the other members of Speakeasy Marketing. Over the years I have tried many different marketing agencies and have felt like I was being taken advantage of. They are amazing. If I have an issue or problem, they quickly responded and did whatever it takes to fix it. Amber has been assigned to my account, and she checks in with me a couple of times a month to see if she can do anything to improve my business. I feel like she really cares about me and wants to make sure that Speakeasy is doing what they promised. Bottom line is, very professional, always keep in contact with me, and most importantly, they are bringing in high quality clients to my firm. I would highly recommend them to anyone. Five Stars all the way!"

— Matt Nebeker, Esq.

****

"My Account Manager Michelle Farrarr was always responsive to anything I asked, was proactive in regularly checking in with me, and was always professional and just a pleasure to deal with."

— Jason Bassett, Esq.

****

"Speakeasy has been a pleasure to work with since I signed up with them many months ago. They have an approach to marketing that is user friendly and promotes long term growth in marketing reach, not just short term. They are friendly, easy to reach and contact, very responsive. While the results are, again, not immediate, I am now seeing unprecedented results, so much in fact that we are having to turn people away at times."

— Tyler Randolph, Esq.

****

"Speakeasy Marketing worked on my website and social media platform(s) and due to their hard work and diligence they helped transform my (previously hidden) site to one that is generating leads. I am being located more easily. The tremendous work they have done helped me stand out in areas of law that many lawyers practice and competition is stiff. I highly recommend using them for marketing if you want your business to grow."

— Mike Barrett, Esq.

****

"I've been in the marketing game for 25 years as a criminal defense attorney. I went through the Yellow Pages and then the Internet when that marketing became popular. I know how Internet marketing works and I've had a lot of success with it. In a big market like Los Angeles, Speakeasy marketing is on the cutting edge as far as Internet marketing goes. They really know what they're doing and they've got their system set up right. If you want a multi prong attack on the Internet that includes a Google, social media and everything in between these guys are the ones to go to. I highly endorse them."

— Ronald Hedding, Esq.

****

"I highly recommend Speakeasy. The particular thing I like about it is that they're holistic. They don't believe in 1 or 2 or 3 methods of marketing - they believe & implement numerous methods. Moreover, they craft their services to your individual needs/wants - unlike others who take cookie-cutter approaches."

— David Bliven, Esq.

****

TABLE OF CONTENTS

SECTION 3:

SECTION 1:

WHY MOST LAWYERS ARE INVISBLE TO AFFLUENT CLIENTS

Do you want to attract more affluent clients in 2021?

People who are used to getting the best of almost everything, who have a complex (i.e. not typical) legal problem, who stand to lose a LOT if they hire a cheaper inexperienced attorney, and who have the means to pay high fees?

If so, I have a message for you. No build up or tease.

I urge you to **flip to page 27**, read carefully, and take careful notes. Because the insights I share could make your year. They're not obvious. And most lawyers, frankly, don't get it — which is why they struggle to attract these clients.

Need more calls? This is your best bet.

A lot of attorneys are thinking about their marketing right now.

About some of the things they can do, things they can invest in — over the next few weeks, months, and year ahead — to really OWN 2021.

Maybe you are too.

If so, I'd be remiss if I didn't share an insight with you.

For than a decade now, we've put food on our families' tables by helping attorneys across almost every practice area attract more of their best cases, grow their bottom line, and, really, build the thriving practice they deserve.

And, as arrogant as this might sound:

If we weren't good at it, we would have starved to death long ago.

We've seen our clients spend, over the years, millions of dollars on all kinds of different media and advertising. Radio ads. Bus stop ads. Billboards. Google and Facebook ads. SEO. Direct mail packages. Paid newspaper articles.

We've sure seen a lot of fads come and go.

There are media that, for a while, were making our clients a LOT of money, that just disappeared and dried up almost overnight. Like Yellow Pages.

And there are some that, for many years, most attorneys treated with disdain, which now no attorney would be caught dead without. Like SEO.

But there's one medium that stands out.

It's the one that, hands down, has been lucrative for almost every single one of our clients who tried it. I would even go as far as to say — that if you want to land more cases, you try this, and it doesn't earn back at least ten times your investment over the next year, there's something seriously wrong.

That's how powerful this medium is.

I use it every year for Speakeasy Marketing.

Sometimes twice per year.

It's easily the best thing I've ever done to attract more and better clients. It's the work horse that has been reliably filling our pipeline for years now.

And, over the last three years, whenever I've launched any kind of project or business venture in another market, it's now the first thing I do.

The attorneys that take my advice and invest in this medium as well — they often end up replicating this two, three, four, sometimes five times.

That's how much of a game-changer it was for them.

What is this medium?

Why is it such a powerful way to attract clients?

And, if it's everything I make it out to be (and it is, plus more), then why isn't every attorney in America using it to build their law practice too?

All good questions.

And I address them in full; all you have to do is **turn to page 34**, and read closely.

Authority positioning vs. UNASSAILABLE authority positioning

You might have heard of Mark Victor Hansen, or Robert Kiyosaki.

And I'm sure you're definitely familiar with Robert Greene — author of *The 48 Laws of Power, The Art of Seduction, Mastery,* and other such titles.

Do you know what these three authors have in common?

(Besides being respected authors who have succeeded in carving out a niche for themselves in one of the only industries more competitive than law...)

They, effectively, "own" a franchise of connected book titles.

Robert Greene is the "dark side of humanity" guy. He wrote the books on power, seduction, war, mastery, and other similar topics. In short, if you want to learn how to be an effective Bond Villain, this guy is your man.

Robert Kiyosaki is the "Rich Dad, Poor Dad" guy. He parlayed a best-selling book into a franchise of related spin-off books. All nowhere near as good as the first, but all cementing his place on a much-coveted pedestal.

And Mark Victor Hansen?

He's the "Chicken Soup for the Soul" guy. Again, he wrote a hit, and had the brains to parlay that into a series of dozen titles — most of which are little more than repackaged versions of his original Chicken Soup for the Soul book, with the addition of a few unique chapters and new intro.

All three are, of course, authority figures.

But they're more than that. In a space where, by definition, every one of their competitors is vying to be the respected guru or expert in a particular field or niche, these three authors have created unassailable authority positioning.

That's why they charge outlandish fees to speak at packed-out events and utter the same old tired platitudes, when hundreds of their competitors would willingly pay for the privilege of speaking to an audience. (This is huge.)

It's why they get invited onto Oprah or Joe Rogan's podcast.

And it's why lucrative deals fall on their lap.

And, do you know what?

You can create the same thing.

You can have this same advantage working for you. A franchise or series of books that gives you undisputed ownership of a specific legal niche.

And still without having to write a single word.

How?

Flip to page 41, and you'll know.

Repurpose your book into a second website?

Some attorneys now have "satellite" websites.

These are second, third, fourth, and, in some cases, fifth websites that complement your practice's main website — by providing information and resources that are specific to a particular legal niche or practice area.

Why bother?

Why go through the trouble of creating more websites?

Because, for attorneys who have already authored a book, it's an easy, low-cost, and effective way to take the content you've already produced and turn it into an online authority platform. A platform that cements your position as the respected authority on these types of cases and attracts quality leads.

There's more:

Because it's a separate website, with its own domain, it's a completely independent online presence. It doesn't affect the SEO rankings or any other aspect of your practice's main website. It's simply another asset you own.

If you're clever about it...

You can fill your new authority website with dozens of written content articles, FAQs, videos, podcast episodes, and other media assets without needing to create ANY new content yourself.

It can all be done by repurposing your book's content.

Look at it from the point of view of an affluent potential:

They get your name from a valued friend or advisor. Someone who says, "Patent attorney? For your new business? Speak to this lady."

When they check you out online and size you up, they see that you not only wrote the book on their particular legal need — you also have a companion website that is filled with articles, videos, podcasts, and other resources.

Your competitor?

All he has is a couple of pages of fluff content on his main website. Nothing that demonstrates how he is the authority on this specific type of case.

Who would you call?

Who would you be willing to pay more to retain?

This is the power of having this kind of "satellite" website.

It's not for every attorney. But, for those who have the stature for this kind of authority positioning, it's a great way to attract new and better clients.

On page 48, I explore the process of building a "satellite" authority platform. And I share some tips for how you can make yours the most SOLID one in your metro/practice area, i.e. what you should include on there.

Find page 48 now, and you'll find everything you need for building your "satellite" authority platform.

Why some attorneys are "crack" to journalists and media hosts

If one of your goals for 2021 is to get your firm featured, quoted, or otherwise mentioned in the media, today's podcast episode is for you.

It's about how to make yourself attractive to journalists/editors.

How to show up on their radar and position yourself as the ONE lawyer and authority figure they want to keep in their pocket. Someone who will instantly add credibility and interest to their stories. Someone who will be an endless gold mine of quotes, authoritative insights, and interesting perspectives.

Rather than just another attorney who wants free publicity.

Because here's the thing:

In today's world, media has become a "winner-takes-all" game. If you have the kind of relationships and position described above, it's a relatively small step to go from one or two media features to being THE face people are used to seeing in multiple newspapers and magazines, and hearing on multiple radio stations, and seeing interviewed in magazines, etc.

How can you create these kinds of relationships?

I'll tell you exactly how — just **turn to page 56**, where you'll find specific tips and strategies for cultivating journalists, editors, and hosts.

An insider tip for getting onto high-value legal podcasts

As you probably know, I love podcasts.

As well as the Secrets of Attorney Marketing Podcast, I host at least five other podcasts across various different industries and fields, which now span more than 2,100 episodes (at the time of my writing this). And I've appeared as a guest on more third-party podcasts than I can remember.

Barely a day goes by when I'm not interviewing a high-profile author, respected scientist, or industry thought leader. Or not being interviewed.

Appearing as a guest expert on someone else's podcast isn't as difficult as you might expect. However, there is a "trick" to it. (You can't just send out an email pitch and hope to land a gig. It doesn't work like that.)

A kind of "insider secret", if you will.

And I'm going to reveal that secret with you in this book. I'll explain how you can find high-value podcasts that your ideal clients listen to and are influenced by — and who you have to reach out to (and how) to get on that podcast as an expert guest.

Ready to learn? Then you're ready to **read page 65.**

Referral stream dried up?

Today, we reach the final step of the Authority Snowball.

That is, the seven-step game plan we've developed to overhaul your law practice's positioning in 2021, build out an online and offline presence that draws affluent potentials to you like a magnet, and — really — leapfrog over cheaper and less experienced competitors in your metro/practice area.

What's the final piece of the puzzle?

Building out an extended network of solid referral partners.

The key word here is "extended". (More on this in a moment.)

Most attorneys agree that referral leads are the best leads you can get. They respect you more. They come prequalified. They are far more likely to close. And they generally become better clients. Easily worth the referral fee.

Most attorneys would give their right arm to get more of them. And many would give their left arm too for a steady, dependable stream of them.

However, the few attorneys who used to enjoy this kind of referral network have seen it get decimated, in some cases annihilated, over the last few years. Their biggest referrers are retiring. And their steam of leads is drying up.

Maybe you're in the same boat.

If so, you'll get a lot out of listening to today's podcast episode.

It's one of the longest — and "meatiest" — episodes that I've recorded in a long time, and it's jam-packed full of insights and actionable advice on how you can leverage some of the authority assets we've talked about over the last few weeks to build a referral network. Not just a network of other lawyers. But a network of advisors, professionals, and other influencers who have the ear of affluent clients — a pool of referrers that is both wider and deeper.

That's what I meant when I said an "extended" referral network.

And, in this book, I'm going to show you how to do it.

Don't wait; dive in, and **head to page 72.**

All 7 lessons: How to attract affluent legal clients

In these pages, I've shared every ingredient in the secret recipe for your Authority Snowball.

Use this recipe to leverage your authority, elevate your positioning, attract affluent clients, and build a formidable practice.

Why affluent clients?

Several reasons:

• They have the means to pay you what you're worth.

• They are culturally conditioned to seek out and value quality, and are generally drawn to the best their money can buy.

• They are investors.

• Their cases are bigger, more complex, and more interesting.

• They have more to lose.

(Not only with the case itself, but more generally. The fallout of a bad outcome on their case or legal situation is far worse for them.)

• They are generally more pleasant to work with.

• They are more sophisticated than your typical "legal consumer", understand the finer nuances of your work, and respect you more.

• They have a greater "lifetime value", simply because they are more likely to require your counsel multiple times over their life.

• Over time, you build a more formidable reputation.

A lot of information has been packed into this one short book. But don't worry, these pages are bound, and they're not going anywhere.

And now that you've absorbed all they have to offer, neither is your Authority Snowball — unless it's picking up speed, and picking up snow.

Along the way, you can be picking up this book. Re-read these words. Reflect on them. And continue to implement them.

One more thing before you go...

A succinct summary of the most critical takeaways of this book is waiting for you in **Section 3**. An easy go-to reference for how to build your Authority Snowball. A positive reminder of why you're doing it...

And all the details of what await you at the finish line.

Enjoy!

And, if you're interested in kick-starting this process by authoring a book, visit https://www.jacobsandwhitehall.com/attorneys/speak-a-book/apply/ or call us at (888) 570-7338.

Section 2:

Find Your Niche, Declare Your Authority

A formidable practice is one that stands out, attracts affluent and well-behaved clients, allows you to command high prices, and ultimately leaves you with a better life than most other attorneys. But I'm not here to continue explaining why every attorney wants this type of practice. I'm here to explain *how* to build this type of practice for yourself.

Let's start by considering the middle class. Some people are moving up into the affluent class, and plenty are moving down into the lower class, meaning the middle class is only shrinking—and at an increasing rate. It's an all-hands-on-deck fight to the death for the remaining middle-class clients.

Should you be in this fight too? Are you willing to fight for clients who are price-sensitive and don't have much at stake?

Or, would you rather put your energy toward attracting more affluent clients who have businesses, multiple houses, commercial licenses, and a good reputation to protect?

The affluent clients are the ones you want — they're the ones every attorney wants, but few are brave enough to consistently go after.

The first step is to declare your authority, which doesn't mean beating your chest and shouting it on a mountaintop. It simply means positioning yourself as an authority within your niche.

Let's explore some possibilities:

If you practice criminal defense, then you might highlight the fact that you've been admitted to practice before federal courts, and you might dedicate a second website or a section of your main website to your accomplishments in that area. If there is anything else that makes you stand out even further, like experience handling death penalty cases, then you could showcase that as well.

If you have an unusual or very specific certification, you want to make it known. In the eyes of affluent clients, this will set you apart from the rest.

Many attorneys veer away from handling sex crime cases. However, there is a lot at stake in these cases, both in terms of money and mandatory jail time, so it's an excellent area of the law to specialize in.

A New Jersey attorney named Ron Mondello specializes in 'crimmigration,' which is where criminal defense and immigration law meet. This is a unique specialty in which Mondello has established himself as an authority, and he's done extremely well as a result.

If you practice family law, then you may want to establish yourself in the niche of high-net-worth divorces. These divorces often involve individuals who have a lot of assets and a personal reputation to protect. They might be successful entrepreneurs or owners of multiple businesses, and their divorce cases might be complicated, involving long-term marriage, children, custody issues, and child or spousal maintenance needs. All of these factors will make the case worth a lot more than a case involving a short-term marriage between people who have no children and no real assets.

You might focus on long-term marriages, father's rights, or mother's rights. You might even call yourself a forensic divorce specialist, meaning that you are good at finding hidden assets that the other party doesn't want your client to know about.

Alternatively, you could sell yourself as a specialist for LGBTQ couples, and focus on one or many of the issues they tend to face in your area.

You might even be THE go-to specialist for people who speak Spanish or Chinese.

If you practice estate planning, you could market yourself as a specialist in handling complex will contests, international trusts, domestic trusts, or special needs trusts. You might focus on representing entrepreneurs, business owners, and other high-net-worth individuals.

Specializing will require more specialized products and attention, but it will earn you quite a bit more money and respect.

If you practice personal injury, your niche might be in high-value trucking accident cases, which pose a number of unique challenges. These cases can involve commercial driver's license (CDL) issues, federal and state trucking regulations, catastrophic injury, and other matters that a lot of personal injury attorneys aren't knowledgeable enough to handle effectively.

In personal injury law alone, there are countless ways to carve out your niche and declare your authority.

If you practice business law, you can focus on corporate bankruptcy and restructuring, the tax-saving method of captive-held insurance companies (CHIC), or tax planning for business owners and high-net-worth individuals.

Whichever type of law you practice, you can set yourself apart by designating yourself as a specialist in a specific area, and declaring your authority.

But this is just the first step. Read on…

Attract the Clients You Need

Who are you attracting? Are those the people you *want* to be attracting? By reviewing the cases and clients you've dealt with over the past couple of years, what can you learn?

You may not see huge skews, but there will be slight skews, and that's okay. For example, if you find that 55% of your clients are women, 53% of them are Hispanic, and 25% of them are recently divorced, then you can make an ideal client avatar from this snapshot.

In other words, you can know that there is a set of client factors that is more likely than not to be found in the type of client you want. The type of client who pays well and doesn't complain about it, listens and follows direction, and never screws up their own case.

If you can manage to make history with a case, such as by finding a new loophole in the law or getting a judge to set a judicial precedent, even better.

Most attorneys don't even know what their ideal client avatar looks like, let alone how to target and get those clients in their office.

You need to determine what your ideal client avatar looks like, think about what's important to those clients, and then make a very targeted appeal to them.

Let's explore further using an example of a real Jacobs & Whitehall author:

Case Study: College Sex Crimes in Upper Michigan

Review of an Ann Arbor, Michigan attorney's cases over the span of a few years yielded an important finding: many college students from affluent, old money families in Upper Michigan were being accused of committing sex crimes on college campuses.

As a consequence, many of these families found themselves scrambling to protect their name and reputation, and willing to do so at any price.

Some of the parents held high-profile positions that were threatened by the accusations against their child, others had spent generations caring for their untarnished reputation, and none of them could afford to hire an attorney who wasn't clearly established as an absolute *expert* in the matter.

With these realizations in mind, the Ann Arbor attorney decided to author a book on the topic in order substantiate his claim to authority in this unique legal niche. The book helped him accomplish just that, and he has since done very well attracting affluent clients in Upper Michigan.

This is just one example of how a real Jacobs & Whitehall author found his niche, and declared his authority in it.

Do you want to attract price shoppers and tire kickers? Or do you want to attract people who can't afford *not* to pay for the best? People that want an attorney who will go to 20 hearings and file stacks of motions, if need be, fighting for every inch of their case.

Affluent people have the means to hire an attorney like this. They don't drive around in KIAs, they drive around in Land Rovers and Mercedes, they live in large houses and nice communities.

They're affluent, and they know it.

They have an image of themselves that demands the best. They see themselves as different from others — as more important than others. And as having special needs that must be dealt with properly.

These are the kind of clients that you want to get. To do so, you first have to figure out your declaration of authority.

We'll help you do this during your initial strategy session with us, and we'll also teach you how to leverage it wisely. It takes about 30 minutes to nail down a solid template for your first declaration of authority...your Speak-a-Book.™

Now is the time. Make this year the most lucrative one yet. Apply to the Speak-a-Book™ program with Speakeasy Marketing, Inc and Jacobs & Whitehall.

PUT THE POWER OF A BOOK BEHIND YOUR DECLARATION OF AUTHORITY

You've found your niche, you've identified your avatar client, and you've declared your authority. Now, you need to put power behind that declaration of authority so that you're not just saying it, but <u>making a case</u> for it.

How can you do this?

I can tell you how I did it: by authoring a book. In fact, I've authored several books, my flagship being *Secrets of Attorney Marketing Law School Dares Not Teach*. This book is in its third edition, and next year it will be in its fourth edition.

This one book represents 70 to 80% of all Speakeasy Marketing's business over the past 11 years. It was the best decision I made, and it has helped the business enjoy tremendous growth. When it comes to establishing authority and authoring books, we've helped nearly 300 attorneys in every practice area you can think of.

The attorneys who authored one or more books with us found that it not only set them apart from the rest of their competitors, but enabled them to attract better clients. The kinds of clients that make for a flourishing practice.

You have to remember that your competitors are attorneys just like you; they passed the bar just like you, they work in the same practice area as you, and they live in the same region as you. In fact, their offices might be down the street from yours, or even in the same office building.

Many of your competitors have decades of experience, and maybe you do too. Some of them are board-certified, and a lot of them are credentialed to the hilt.

It's very difficult for potential clients to determine from an online ad which attorney in their area is better than all the others. They will compare your Avvo rating versus everyone else's, and in the end, they're simply not going to know who to choose.

Unless, of course, they dig deep, but not many of them are going to do that.

<u>A book throws down the gauntlet.</u> It busts through the internet ads and ratings and comes to the forefront of their screens and minds. A book sets you apart from your competitors precisely how you want it to.

In the US alone, there are about one million attorneys, and solo and small firms account for about 400,000 to 500,000 of those, at least. We've worked with 300 of them, which is nothing.

Don't Get Mired Down by Misconceptions

Not enough time, takes too much effort, not going to be helpful…these are the **misconceptions** that prevent those other attorneys from authoring a book.

I and the hundreds of attorneys we've helped author a book can tell you what a significant impact their book had on their practice. Just consider the Katz & Phillips firm in Orlando, Florida: they chose to author five books with Speakeasy Marketing, and it only took about six months for them to make back **TEN TIMES** the amount of money they spent.

Some of their books have been out there for years now, and they've likely made <u>100 times or more</u> what they paid. The books have served them extremely well.

Distribute Your Authority

Some attorneys hand out their books to bail bondsmen, who aren't allowed to recommend a specific attorney, but are allowed to put attorneys' books out in their offices for anyone to pick up and thumb through.

Have your secretaries offer a print or digital version to every person who calls your office. Have photos taken of yourself holding the book, surrounded by stacks of other books. This will demonstrate your authority in a powerful, *powerful* way.

Many attorneys also give copies of their book to auto shops, pain doctors, and CPAs...it all depends on what area of law they practice, and which locations are most likely to work with their ideal client.

An attorney's book can be given to every potential client who walks through the doors of their practice. And the really smart attorneys will even mail a copy of their book to potential clients, along with an electronic copy for easy access. Send the whole book, or digital copies of a few chapters that pertain to the potential client's specific issue.

A book can even be used to land news interviews, blog features, and speaking engagements.

Imagine hearing...

"Hey, I thumbed through your book, and I was really impressed...I think you can help me with my case."

And...

"I read your book cover to cover. Thank you. You answered a lot of questions I had. Can you help me?"

These are direct quotes that attorneys have received from clients. Wouldn't it be great if you started hearing the same thing, from the types of clients you truly want to work for?

We've made it so that you can, and without spending much of your time—about **three hours in total**.

Here's how it works:

During the first 90-minute phone interview with Tracy Merda, the head of Jacobs & Whitehall, you'll be able to identify your ideal avatar client and determine the topic of your book.

We have libraries of thousands of questions for each practice area in the metro, and Tracy will help you choose the best ones for your practice, tailoring them to your preferences. Your answers to these questions will be recorded, transcribed, edited, and put into book format. This means that within just 90 minutes of your time, we'll extract loads of valuable content—enough content to make the book that will put power behind your declaration of authority.

At Jacobs & Whitehall, we will make the cover, inserts, and overall layout of the book, and then get it ready for release on Amazon and Kindle.

Once we send you the final draft, you'll spend an hour or so looking through it and making sure everything is precisely how you want it. Does it contain all the content you want it to? Does it flow the way you imagined it would? If not, we'll fix it until it's perfect in your eyes.

Interested in an audiobook version? No problem, we can make that happen. We can make an e-cover that you can put on your website, along with a link to a free download. All that potential clients will need to do is enter their name, phone number, and email address.

And guess what that does? It generates more leads for you.

We'll print and ship 100 copies to you for about $5 per book including shipping, which is an incredible price.

And at about 65 pages, your book will be a concise, easy read.

It will be self-published through Speakeasy Publishing online at Jacobs & Whitehall, and available on Amazon and Kindle, as well as Audible if you choose.

Everyone loves to get Amazon packages; send your potential clients a copy of your book directly from Amazon. They're going to be impressed.

The goal is to maximize return on investment. If within the first year you are not getting three to 10 times your money back and you've earnestly tried to get your book into the right hands, then something is terribly wrong.

Most of the attorneys who author a book with us experience a great return on it, and they come back for a second, third, fourth, and fifth book.

I highly encourage you to consider what a difference this could make in your practice, and in your life as a whole.

This is THE critical step in the seven steps Authority Snowball. Author a book. You'll be pleased that you did.

Schedule a strategy session with us today. Call (888) 225-8594 and visit jacobsandwhitehall.com to learn more.

ELEVATE YOUR AUTHORSHIP, ELEVATE YOUR AUTHORITY

You've authored your first book. Now what? How do you take things to the next level? How do you ensure that your position of authority is unassailable, even if nearby competitor attorneys have *also* authored a book?

The key is to elevate your authorship by establishing a *series* of books. Regardless of how well your first book is working for you, it might be very niched and leave several aspects of your practice unspoken for. That's perfectly okay. In fact, that's what makes your book ripe for expansion into a series.

We have a program for that. With just <u>one extra 90-minute interview</u>, we make two additional books so that you'll have a suite of <u>three</u>.

By retaining about 80% of the content in the first book, and adding some new content and customizations, you end up with a series of books.

Consider the *Chicken Soup for the Soul* books. After Mark Victor Hansen wrote the first book, he used it as a template for writing dozens of other books, like *Chicken Soup for the Young Person's Soul*, *Chicken Soup for the Old Soul*, *Chicken Soup for the LGBT Soul*, *Chicken Soup for the Entrepreneur's Soul*, and on and on.

In each book, about 80 to 90% of the content is the same. By adding a new chapter or two and customizing each book, he has authored multiple books and established a franchise.

What effect does this have on readership?

It makes even the most diverse readership feel as though something has been crafted uniquely for them. It makes them feel as though the books are speaking to them, about them, and for them.

This is how a troubled teenager who picks up *Chicken Soup for the Teenager's Soul* is going to feel, it's how an entrepreneur who picks up *Chicken Soup for the Entrepreneur's Soul* is going to feel, and the list goes on.

What effect does this have more broadly?

It makes it easier for people to recognize you and your work. To recognize your **authority.**

Almost everyone has heard of the *Chicken Soup for the Soul* book series, because there are so many of them and because the series has become so popular. It's been marketed and promoted so well in so much media that nearly everyone knows about it.

The same can be said about Robert Kiyosaki's *Rich Dad Poor Dad* book, which led to a series of books and related products, all which further solidified his recognizability and authority.

The point is this: If you make extra editions of your first book and develop a themed series, you will garner much more attention and recognition.

And when you do this, each individual book in your series will promote the others. A rise in tide lifts all books. The more books you have, the more likely it is that people are going to be impressed by you.

You are no longer just an author, but an author of **three, five, ten, or even more books.**

I can personally speak to the success of this strategy, because I've done it myself. I've authored *Secrets of Attorney Marketing Law School Dares Not Teach*, *The Attorney Authority Reboot*, *12 Powerful Principles of Prosperous Law Practices,* and a soon-to-be-released book on Speakeasy Marketing's Virtual Closing System. I've also authored a book on DUI that features insights from many DUI attorneys, and one on online marketing featuring Perry Marshall, a true marketing guru.

The more books I put out, the greater the positive effect. I'm getting more attention; people will buy one book, learn of the many other subjects I cover in other books, and then buy one of those too. Ultimately, this is helping me attract a lot more clients to Speakeasy Marketing and Jacobs & Whitehall.

In other words…

I eat my own dog food.

I practice what I preach and I encourage you to do the same, because this is what will <u>elevate your AUTHORITY</u>.

Let's break it down a little more:

What does it really look like to author multiple books that all carry the same theme?

If you practice DUI law, you could author a series of DUI books, with each book addressing a different subcategory of DUI:

- ✓ DUI with high BAC

- ✓ DUI with illegal or prescription drugs

- ✓ DUI involving a car accident

- ✓ DUI with commercial driver's license

- ✓ DUI for under 21

- ✓ DUI for under 18

- ✓ DUI with a child in the car

✓ DUI with bodily injury

For DUI alone, there are probably 20+ permutations you can take advantage of.

If you practice personal injury law with a focus on auto accidents, you could author a series of auto accident books, with each book addressing a different type of accident:

✓ Accidents with fatalities

✓ Accidents with uninsured drivers

✓ Catastrophic auto accidents

✓ Trucking accidents

✓ Bicycle accidents

✓ Motorcycle accidents

✓ Accidents involving pedestrians

For auto accidents alone, there is a long list of specific topics that you can expand upon in a book.

If you practice estate planning, you could author a series of estate planning books, with each book addressing a different estate planning need or circumstance:

✓ Wills

✓ Will contests

- ✓ Special needs trusts

- ✓ Irrevocable trusts

- ✓ Revocable trusts

- ✓ Minimizing estate tax

- ✓ Long-term care planning

It doesn't matter the practice area, there are many different types of books you can author, and that's what we want to help you accomplish through our Speak-a-Book™ Platinum program.

If you've already done one Speak-a-Book™, then you'll enjoy special pricing, and only have to commit 90 more minutes of your time to turn your first book into your first book *series*.

This is a fantastic way to **accelerate your authority** and make you **unstoppable**.

One more example before you go:

There's a fellow named Alan Weiss, the Million Dollar consultant guy...He has Million Dollar Consulting, Million Dollar Speaking, Million Dollar Consulting Proposals, etc.

He *is* the Million Dollar brand.

And you can make a brand for your law firm, regardless of what type of law you practice.

The more books you author, the better your ability to create a common theme...recognizable books with similar colors and a similar feel.

This will powerfully amplify your presence and place you above any level of competition. It will magnify, augment, and accelerate your success. Big time.

You might already be a Jacobs & Whitehall client, you might not be — it doesn't matter.

Because if you're interested, all you have to do is contact Tracy Merda. You'll speak with her or Dennis, a top Speak-a-Book™ consultant.

With a 30-minute strategy session, you'll learn how to create a series of books tailored to your practice. One that highlights everything you want clients to know.

Call (888) 225-8594, and visit
https://www.jacobsandwhitehall.com/ or
https://www.speakeasymarketinginc.com/.

ABOVE AND BEYOND BOOKS: BUILD YOUR ONLINE MULTIMEDIA PLATFORM

At this point, you may have already authored not only your first book, but your first book series. This means you are well on your way to raising your authority to the highest level.

This chapter is dedicated to showing you how to move above and beyond books, to an **authoritative online multimedia platform**. One that establishes a formidable online presence. One that demands respect, and continues to attract the clients you seek.

This can be accomplished by capitalizing on the work you've already done, and it's really quite simple.

What we'll do is help you make the move *from book to satellite web page*, where you share the basics of your practice and personal or professional background, tell potential clients how to contact you, and reap every last benefit of the books you've authored.

A satellite web page for your book will be dedicated to highlighting the contents of that book, and can feature a picture of you alongside your book, further imprinting a picture of authority in the minds of ideal potential clients. It can also include Amazon, Kindle, and Audible links for easy access.

Do you recall the case study from chapter one?

…An Anne Arbor, Michigan attorney, upon review of his cases over the prior couple of years, identified a very particular legal niche that he'd already established himself in; he just needed to make his authority in it known. And the best way to do that?

That's right, you already know: Author a book. Once completing his book on college sex crimes in Anne Arbor, this attorney could choose to stop. But stopping there would mean limiting his reach into success.

The other option? Create a satellite website based on the book. This satellite web page would have no negative impact on the existing main site in terms of SEO. In fact, including a link on the satellite site directing people to the main site would only drive more traffic to the main site, and attract more ideal avatar clients.

Creating satellite websites in this way creates a greater web presence and another place to exclusively showcase your authority surrounding each book.

Whether the site features a few chapters or all of the content from one book, it would offer potential clients another way to access the material.

And this would be an optimal place to post:

- ✓ Updates in the law that relate to the cases at hand

- ✓ New information about the current state of the legal niche

- ✓ Bonus commentary

- ✓ Testimonials

- ✓ Case results that pertain specifically to an aspect of the book

Feature Testimonials on Your Satellite Web Page

Let's say you've authored a book on DUI, which includes a chapter on multiple DUI defense. And maybe you've helped clients get a huge break on a third, fourth, or even fifth DUI charge. If so, there would be no place better to include testimonials from those clients than on your satellite web page, because the testimonials will relate directly to the material in your book.

This is a very powerful way of amplifying your authority.

From Book to Email Series and Blog Articles

We've helped a number of our attorney authors repurpose the content from their book into an email series that gets sent to potential clients.

And what has this accomplished for those attorney authors? A reintegration of their book, and a re-establishment of their authority.

The spoon-feed strategy was used on me, and it worked:

A long time ago, I bought a book from an online marketer by the name of Perry Marshall.

Shortly after, I started getting emails, and they'd read something like, *"People have a lot of questions about Chapter 3. Let's pick apart some of the issues here."*

Via email, Perry Marshall effectively spoon-fed me passages and bits of the book.

Sure, at first, I thought it was weird. But then I realized it was effective nonetheless: I was consuming more and more of the book's content, and becoming more and more absorbed by it.

At that point, it didn't matter if I put the book away for a few days or weeks, because the emails drew me back every time.

It was a great way of driving the engagement between me and Perry Marshall, while at the same time further establishing his authority.

And now? <u>I've been a customer of his for about a decade</u>. It obviously worked. And it worked really well.

The same thing can be done with your books. All you have to do is spoon-feed compelling and important information to potential clients via email, using the content you've *already created*.

Your book's content can also be repurposed as **blog articles on your satellite website**.

This will keep it fresh, and keep those search engine spiders crawling.

If a potential client has a case that falls in the practice area covered in your book, have your admins refer them to your satellite website, which is sure to impress.

This is very important, and it will help you more than you might think.

Inside the Minds of Potential Clients

What's going on inside the mind of someone who encounters this?

To answer this question, first you have to step back and consider that most attorneys look the same, sound the same, smell the same. They say the same things. They've been in practice for years and years, they "fight" for their clients, they're "compassionate" and they offer "unmatched legal expertise."

But you see, those are just words. And by using the same ones, all you're going to do is end up in the same category as your competitors, and at the mercy of chance.

But what if you have a book series, and a satellite website dedicated to each book in it, and an email series that spoon-feeds valuable content, and blogs with information on the very latest in your legal niche, and testimonials from other people who've been where your ideal client IS, and who benefitted from hiring YOU. Not the attorney down the street, not the one a few blocks over, and not the many other attorneys in your region who practice the same type of law.

YOU offer potential clients an <u>entire set of authority artifacts</u> that reinforces and amplifies who you are in their mind.

THIS is what will help you attract affluent, high-end clients. The types of clients that will make your practice more **profitable** than it's ever been.

And because you've demonstrated unquestionable authority in the area of law specific to their issue, they will respect you. They will respect you simply because your authority radiates from you.

At Speakeasy Marketing and Jacobs & Whitehall, we utilize these strategies to cement our position of authority in the attorney marketing world. We post blog articles, we send emails and promotions, we deliver you — and all other potential clients — the information you need to know about the Speak-a-Book™ process.

Some of you have been on my list for years and years. And I can't tell you how many times I've heard a permutation of this sentiment:

"How do you guys put out all this content? It's crazy good, and I love it. I've been following you for years."

We practice what we preach because it works.

We constantly have to reassert and reaffirm our authority in your mind and the minds of other attorneys, because we want you as a client. In fact, I'm doing it right now, as I create the content for this book.

You can do the same to further amplify your books and your platform.

Some people like to read, some like to listen, and some like to watch. What do your clients prefer? There's no way to know, so your best bet is to provide every avenue of learning. We help our clients cater to the preferences of *their* clients, by turning their wealth of knowledge and expertise into books, audiobooks, podcasts, and videos.

You want to be firing on all cylinders. You want to disseminate your information in every way possible so that you can capture all learning styles, and as a result, capture more clients.

Be Authoritatively Ubiquitous

Whether it's Google, Yelp, Amazon, Audible, or any other media outlet, we'll help get your reviews out there.

The more reviews you have in more places, the more often people will perceive you as being <u>everywhere</u>, as being ten times as big as you are.

People like Suzie Norman and Dr. Phil and all other famous "advice-givers" aren't found on just one platform. They're found everywhere.

When your declaration of authority shows up everywhere, it'll multiply the impact of your online presence and generate significantly more business for you.

Author a book, and then a series of books. Then, use that content to create satellite websites for posting blog articles, podcasts, videos, and audio versions of particular chapters or topics.

And as always, get your reviews on every platform possible.

It's incredibly powerful, and we're here to assist every step of the way.

We can help you become authoritatively ubiquitous through the Authority Platform upgrade. If you're interested, call us at (888) 225-8594, email <u>support@speakeasymarketinginc.com</u>, or visit <u>https://www.jacobsandwhitehall.com/</u>.

If you engage in this and commit to it, you're going to be leaps and bounds ahead of other attorneys. I can't recommend it highly enough.

DON'T CHASE THE MEDIA: LET IT CHASE YOU

Pretty much everyone wants to be featured in the media, and I'll admit it, I'm no exception. Why?

It's because I understand the value in it. Not only does a third-party media feature fortify your authority and extend your reach to a much wider clientele base, but it ultimately translates to a more lucrative practice for years to come.

You're probably thinking that it's a feat too great to achieve, given the sheer number of people who may want it just as badly as you. But the scale is balanced by an equally strong hunger for new and compelling content on the part of the media. They have a never-ending hole that they have to fill for news, cable, blogs, podcasts, etc. And in their attempts to put out the best content, they are relentless.

So, how do you make sure you get in the media when you otherwise wouldn't?

First, you need to know that it's a winner-takes-all phenomenon. Journalists go after the hottest, most authoritative experts. They're after quotes and opinions and insights that will lead to a story that makes *them* stand out.

Journalists will beat down doors to get at this content, while at the same time ignoring calls from self-proclaimed "experts" who are just seeking publicity.

How do you become the person that they're chasing?

We'll get into that momentarily…

Before we do, I want you to understand the importance of strategy. If you want to be the media's darling, you have to be attractive — attractive as an authoritative expert.

Up until this point, we've covered four steps to creating your authority snowball:

1. Identify your ideal avatar client and declare your authority.

2. Author a book.

3. Author a series of books.

4. Turn your book into a powerful online authority platform that includes everything from podcasts, blog articles, and videos to satellite websites and reviews.

Now, just taking the first two steps is an excellent start, because it'll raise your positioning over your competitors and give you an edge.

But, if you're in a competitive space, then you're probably going to need all four of these things in order to really catch the attention of the media. Once you've checked off numbers one through four, it's going to be a lot easier, because your omnipresence will not only impact potential clients, but the media too. It will impress them, showcase your abilities, and make it clear that you're the expert they need to hear from.

All this, though, still isn't enough. And here I get to the meat of the matter.

There are **two instrumental steps to getting featured in the media**, and doing it the _right_ way.

There is a nature to the game, one that Dr. Seuss could explain: You stand on one turtle to stand on the next turtle to stand on the one after that and on and on until one day…you're Yertle the turtle: you're standing on a thousand turtles, with the best and highest vantage point possible.

We'll get to that vantage point, but we have to start from the bottom.

Step #1: Getting in the Media

Getting featured in the media is about positioning. A lot of attorneys do this half-heartedly, and that's a big mistake. They'll send an email or a fax or maybe even a letter to an editor, and when they don't hear back, they settle into the idea that it's too competitive or just not in the cards for them.

Half-hearted doesn't work.

You have to identify the type of media relevant to what you do, and contact as many people within that realm as possible.

If you practice criminal defense, don't waste your time contacting sports or family media. You've got to find media relevant to what you do, whether that's estate planning, business law, DUI, domestic violence, family law, or personal injury.

Which media report on things that fall into your area of expertise? How do they report? Who does the reporting? Are they on YouTube? Are they on mainstream media? If Joe Johnson is the one who always covers the major car crashes and personal injuries, and if you practice personal injury law, then Joe Johnson is the person you want to go after.

And then, you want to find that same Joe Johnson in other publications. Don't waste your time contacting a whole bunch of irrelevant media people.

Diligence Pays

Once you've identified and contacted your Joe Johnson is every publication you can, you <u>must </u>follow up. Everyone is busy these days, especially people in the media, yet they are constantly thinking about what content they'll put out the next day or week.

They focus on the short-term picture, not the long-term one, so you have to follow up. There's no way around it.

If I emailed potential clients once and never again, I would be dead broke and have no business. I email multiple times a week, for days, weeks, months, years at a time. I also mail materials and hold special promos, on a never-ending basis.

I've been doing this for 11 years now, and I get emails and calls from attorneys all the time who say, *"Rich, I've been on your list for six months, something has come up, and I'm interested in talking to you."*

Or…*"Hey, Rich. I've been on your list for years. We were loving our SEO provider, but they went out of business and I want to talk to you."*

So many of my current clients followed me for months or years before finally becoming ready to press "Go."

If I hadn't kept up with these people like I did, I would have a tiny fraction of the business I have now.

It's really pretty simple: To get what you want, you have to follow up to the end of time.

If you do this, you will start to see results. You may have to change tactics and adjust your strategy, but without follow-up, you'll think wrongly that it doesn't work. This does work.

What We Offer

We can help you make a list of media platforms that are relevant to you AND your ideal prospects, because those prospects will consume the same media that you'll soon be featured in.

Next, we'll help you send a **letter of introduction** to the right people at these media companies. This is a crucial step that has to be taken carefully.

What do I mean by that?

You want to craft an impressive letter and intro package that includes a picture of you, your talking points, a link to and picture of your book(s), and all of your authority assets, like your main website, satellite book websites, podcasts, blog articles, accolades, and more.

In the letter, you provide a concise summary of who you are, what you do, what you've accomplished, and where to find all of your authority assets. Include that you're available to provide quotes, opinions, and/or legal facts on your topics of expertise, and offer to write a guest column or make a guest appearance on TV or radio.

Once you send out your letter of introduction, we'll follow up. If there's a bite and people are interested in hearing more, we can send them an electronic version of your book for free, or we can mail them a physical copy of your book.

*Note: It's not necessary for them to read your book cover to cover. They can thumb through it, and it'll do its job, because it will still impress them and convey your authority.

In fact, clients tell us all the time that they were hired after prospective clients flipped through their book or read one or two chapters. No need to read every word. Some people will consume all of it and some won't, and that's okay; it will still affect them positively.

Now, you don't want to hit your sought-after media people with the same material again and again. You want to do it strategically. First you send the letter, and if you get an electronic response, try sending your book a week or two later, followed by a podcast or blog article.

It's the Chinese water torture way of disseminating your authority assets...*a drop at a time, until one day, they're ready for you.*

But in order for it to work, those droplets have to be delivered consistently. And if you do this, they are going to be much more likely to call you when a relevant story is breaking. This might happen a month or a year after you first contact them, but rest assured that when the right story breaks, they're going to remember you.

And when they do remember you, they'll call you. **Suddenly, you'll have landed your first third-party media feature.**

This is not rocket science, but it does require that you have the right things in place, which is where 99.9999% of attorneys go wrong. They might author a book or make a few attempts at showcasing their authority here and there, but they stop short of leveraging their authority to the max.

Step #2: Staying in the Media

Most of your work is done. You've landed your first media feature, and if all you want is the temporary windfall of business and credibility that comes with it, then your work *is* done.

But to not build upon all the work you've already done would be a mistake you don't want to make.

You can use your media feature for everything it's worth by emphasizing it on your website with just a few words, like *"As Seen on CBS"* (or NBC, or ABC, or Forbes, or wherever you were featured). Continue to leverage your media feature by posting pictures or screenshots of your contribution to the media.

Once you have this, reaching out to more media outlets will be much more fruitful, because there will be evidence that one media outlet has already trusted you and benefitted from your authority. As a result, media outlets will be much more likely to want to interview you, which will build upon and further back your declaration of authority.

Once you get a little bit of media coverage, keep going.

Envision yourself in the near future, being featured in the New York Times, Washington Post, and other well-respected media. Before too long, you'll have a whole list of media logos on your site, boosting your credibility.

And what effect will this have on your ability to attract your ideal avatar client? **A tremendous and lucrative one.** You can send your book to potential clients like you have been, but this time, it can include media logos and "as seen on" stickers.

This is the opposite of a downward vicious cycle: it's the upward virtuous cycle that builds upon itself and continues to grow, where the media become the lights and guardrail of your authority platform, adding to the perception of true prestige.

This will increase your fan base of clients above and beyond that of your competitors. And good luck to them, because your authority is going to pervade everything you do.

Ready to get started?

Call us at (888)225-8594, visit https://www.speakeasymarketinginc.com/ or https://www.jacobsandwhitehall.com/. You can also email us at support@speakeasymarketinginc.com.

This is going to be a game-changer for you and your practice.

BE HEARD ON HIGH-VALUE LEGAL PODCASTS

Podcasting has been around for a fair number of years, but it's grown tremendously, especially over the past year or two.

Joe Rogan, who was the host on Fear Factor, is now the number one podcaster in the world. For close to $200 million, he signed a deal with Spotify for them only to host his podcasts. He is a massive force in the world of podcasts. Sean Carroll, the big-name quantum physicist, and Neil deGrasse Tyson are just a couple of the guests he's had on his show.

Tim Ferris of *The 4-Hour Workweek* has been competing with (his friend) Joe Rogan for the number one podcast, which he's accomplished off and on over the years. About two years ago, Ferris's podcast surpassed about 100 million downloads.

There are many great podcasters out there. I'm not one of the best, but it's clear that I love podcasts. I host an attorney marketing podcast, as well as one on science and health, and at the current rate, I'll have done about 3,000 episodes by the end of 2021.

I've done this for so long and have talked with so many people, and I can tell you that this medium can convey *a lot* of stardom.

Podcasts are big business, and a lot of the major media companies are investing in them.

The point of this chapter is to not only help you understand the **value of landing an interview on the right podcast**, but to help you accomplish this so that the **authority surrounding your Speak-a-Book™** just **continues to grow**.

So, how do you land your <u>first</u> podcast appearance?

I'll start by telling you how it's *not* done: by making a list of podcasters and just telling them, *"Hey, I want to be on your show."*

Podcasters get lots of requests from people, many of which come through email, and offer only a long, droning 10 or 12 sentences about how great they are and why they should be invited as a guest. The people who send these requests don't even look to see whether the podcast is relevant to what they do, and they don't specify their talking points.

If you want to use a podcast appearance to further amplify your authority and boost your Speak-a-Book(s)™, then you have to do a couple of things:

#1 Build a list of relevant podcasters.

If you do estate planning, you may want to tie this to wealth preservation, tax issues, trusts, etc., and believe me, there are people who are doing podcasts on these topics.

If you practice criminal defense, look into the many true crime podcasts. These may be very appropriate, because…well because what's more true crime than the details of true criminal cases, spoken by an attorney?

If you've handled some high-level or really interesting cases, you probably have the juicy stuff that true crime podcasters (and their listeners) want to hear (of course, you would change the names and some of the facts of each case to protect client confidentiality).

Within every market, whether it's divorce, child custody, personal injury, DUI, etc., there are legal issues that are pervasive in society, and famous people aren't immune to them. There is a lot of material to be explored, and a lot of podcasters who are looking for experts on that material.

You just have to start by identifying the podcasters relevant to what you do.

#2 Present and prepare yourself in the right way.

You will need a one-sheet, which is a single-page document that showcases YOU.

It should include a professional picture of yourself and of your book, talking points, links to your websites, and a list of any media outlets you've already appeared on.

This will make a much better impression on relevant podcasters than an email wherein you just blab about some cliché that you think will earn you points (I get a lot of those).

It's okay to reach for the lower-level podcasters first. Every podcaster needs interviewees, and every media outlet always needs new content.

So, get after them. Dip your toe in the podcast world before diving straight in, because if you haven't been interviewed before, it might take you a little time to get used to. And that's true regardless of how many times you've cross-examined people in court with no fear. That doesn't always translate to being interviewed on a podcast.

From experience, I can tell you that some people are great to interview, some don't answer a single question I ask them. Some are boring, some are terse, some will talk you to death.

And lastly on this topic, **be patient**. It might take a little time to land an interview on the right podcast.

Podcasts: More Than What Meets the Ear

A lot of podcasters use video, which means their podcasts aren't just heard, but seen on YouTube and many different media channels.

They are promoted on Twitter, Facebook, and especially Facebook Live.

With the popularity of Zoom these days, chances are your podcast interview will be in video format, which will give people a chance to see you and get a feel for whether you're likable.

Once you do land a podcast interview, use it for everything it's worth. And by that, I mean post it on your website, include the podcaster's badge on your website, and make it known that the *world of podcasting has invited you in,* **because of your authority**.

The more accolades you can include on your website, the more respect you will garner from potential clients.

They're going to think, *"Wow, this lawyer is in the news, they've been on a podcast, they have a radio show, they've done books...I don't know if I can afford this person."*

They're going to assume that you charge a lot of money, and to the affluent client who you really want, this will actually make you *more* appealing.

Top-tier, well-respected, authoritative attorneys are who the affluent clients go after, cost aside.

Know the Podcaster Mindset

Be prepared to ask, *"What kind of listeners do you have, and what message can I bring that will be really valuable to them?"*

Tell the podcaster that your goal is to make your guest appearance a home run for the podcaster AND their listeners. Find out how to make those **listeners *love* what you have to say**.

A podcaster who hears that is going to realize that you truly care about adding value to the lives of their listeners, and as a result, will immediately find you more respectable than almost every other person who requests to be on their show.

Maximize the Value of Your Podcast Interview

Once you are invited as a podcast guest, you can offer listeners a coupon for a free consultation or a percentage off any retainer agreement.

Your fees don't have to be set in stone. You can be flexible with this. You can easily add 10% to your fee, and then "discount" it in the way you see fit.

The purpose of this is to say "Thank you" to listeners.

When I do this, my listeners love it. They think, *"Wow, Rich not only does this podcast, but he gets us discounts on stuff that he helps us learn about. This is great."*

You can ensure that the listeners of your episode(s) have similar thoughts, which will drive more of the *right* type of business your way.

The Legal Thought Leaders Network Podcast

I want to help you enter the world of podcasts, which is why I've recently launched the Legal Thought Leaders Network Podcast, where I'll interview attorneys four times per quarter for their specific metro and practice area.

If you choose to take advantage of this, you can use your appearances as accolades on your website.

It's not expensive.

And I'll help you repurpose the content you provide, such as by transcribing and editing your interviews so that they can be posted as articles on your site. This will boost your SEO, and improve client engagement.

Find out more about the Legal Thought Leaders Podcast Network by visiting https://www.speakeasymarketinginc.com/, calling (888) 225-8594, or emailing us at support@speakeasymarketinginc.com.

EXTEND YOUR NETWORK OF SOLID REFERRAL PARTNERS

Every attorney I know loves referrals because they are the best leads. They have little price resistance, and they are preconditioned to respect you and want to work with you.

Why?

Because they've been referred by someone they trust, like a colleague, family member, or friend.

However, most attorneys I know have also told me that their referral stream has dried up, and they don't know how to get things flowing again.

At least 95% of attorneys have no system for attracting referrals. It just happens or doesn't happen. They get them or they don't get them.

And guess what? This mindset won't work.

Not only do you need a system for attracting referrals, you need the right *kind* of system, one that heeds this reality: These days, about 80% of people use their smartphone to search for attorneys. Long gone are the days of the Yellow Pages, and even the use of desktop computers is on its way out.

The convenience of mobile fits in a front pocket. People fall asleep with their phones beside them, they wake up and start scrolling. At any moment of any day, they can pull out their phone, search the word "attorney", and instantly find dozens and dozens of them.

This makes it very difficult to stand out, and also to get referrals. People not only want, but *expect* immediate solutions to their problems. They aren't willing to wait.

This does NOT mean you can't get a significant amount of business from referrals, it just means that you have to change your approach to fit the modern era.

And what does that really mean? It means you need to **build a referral network.**

Let's break this into two parts:

Part 1: Who is in YOUR Referral Network?

✓ **Past clients** who were happy with the representation you provided. They have family members, friends, coworkers, spouses, etc. who could all become your next client.

However, you can't just assume that past clients will refer you. **Past clients must be cultivated**. If you played a positive role in a past client's life, your work isn't done. You still need to show up in their life every month or so, whether through a newsletter or email or other means, because this is what will ensure that they'll remember YOU.

I've been in business for 12 years now, and I know attorneys in pretty much every state in the country. Naturally, when conversation with a friend, family member, colleague, or acquaintance leads to mention of a past legal case — which it inevitably does — I can't help but say, *"Oh, who represented you? I might know them."*

And guess what I hear 99.99999% of the time? *"Oh, I don't remember their name."*

If your past clients don't remember you, is that your fault?

No, it's not. Because as an attorney, you help people through some of the darkest and most negative times of their lives. You all are champions, and I have a lot of respect for you.

But human nature dictates that bad memories are better off forgotten. And unfortunately, the consequence of that is that you too will be pushed to the periphery of past client memories. Not because they don't like you or because you did a bad job, but simply because they don't want to think about the legal issue which drove them to hire you in the first place.

And because during that time, through no fault of your own, they came to equate hearing from you with negativity. With bad news. Or stressful news. Or just something new that they would have to add to their already long "to-do" list.

Understanding this is key to using past clients as a resource for referrals.

Because once you understand this, you can figure out how to mitigate this negativity. You can show them that hearing from you doesn't have to mean feeling bad or anxious. You can send them a monthly newsletter with positive, uplifting, and informative content.

I can teach you how to do this. And I can show you the importance of doing it often enough to make an impact. Not yearly, not even quarterly. You want to do this monthly.

Why?

Think about any relationship you have in your life. What differentiates a close friend from an acquaintance? In most cases, it's the frequency with which you hear from them.

Would you try to have a relationship with your spouse once a quarter or once a year?

Hopefully not.

And the same idea can be applied to past clients and other referral sources, which we'll get to soon. You need to maintain a continuous, ongoing relationship with your past clients by sending them a newsletter every month.

If this ends up costing you $1.25 per past client per month, that's $18 per year, per past client. And if there are 18 past clients that you're sending your newsletter to, then you would be spending $1,800 per year.

Well, guess what? A **single case** that comes from these efforts is likely to offset the cost you put into it. And by taking this approach, chances are you'll end up with *more* than just one referral per year.

Regularly communicating with past clients is super important.

✓ **Other attorneys** who practice similar or potentially related types of law. I've learned over time that different practice areas are complementary to each other.

Unfortunately, people dealing with divorce may end up in bankruptcy. They may resort to domestic violence because of their frustration. They may need their estate plan revised because there's a break in the family and things are changing.

If someone is dealing with bankruptcy, it may lead to divorce, or the unintentional commission of a crime.

If someone has been in an auto accident and can't work, they could find themselves in bankruptcy, or a divorce due to financial strain.

Every practice area has related practice areas within which the attorneys can be a significant source of referrals.

For example, if you are a family law attorney in Kansas City, then you should network with attorneys in Kansas City who deal with bankruptcy, estate planning, criminal defense, and other types of law. Those attorneys are not competitors; they simply have clients whose needs may overlap with the services that you and your (soon-to-be) referral attorneys provide.

You should identify these attorneys and communicate with them on a monthly basis, just like you should with past clients.

✓ **Businesses and various professionals,** depending on the type of law you practice.

If you're a business lawyer, you should contact all of the small businesses in your area to let them know that if they need advice on licensing requirements or state and city health requirements, or if they want help taking on a new business partner, obtaining key person insurance, negotiating a commercial lease, or dealing with any other business matter that arises, you are there to help them.

Whether you practice family law, criminal defense, estate planning, employment law, or any other type of law, you can take advantage of this strategy, because businesses are composed of people who have the same legal issues as anyone else.

If you're a personal injury lawyer, contact auto repair and body shops, as well as pain doctors and chiropractors.

If you do estate planning, you may want to establish and maintain communication with CPAs, tax attorneys, and other tax professionals.

If you practice criminal defense, you can contact bail bondsmen and leave them with your contact information, or better yet, a copy of your Speak-a-Book™ that they can display in their office.

If you actively curate and cultivate a network of people who know about you and hear from you every month, guess what's going to happen?

Problems will strike and they're going to be much more likely to contact you than just blindly Google someone else.

Your referral network can be big, comprised of thousands of people. But you have to think about the big picture in order to identify who could potentially refer you.

From experience, I can tell you that some of the people who you think will be your best referral sources won't refer you once, and someone who you would never even think of as a referral source might refer you over and over again. That's just how it is, so you want to cultivate a big, broad referral network.

Lavish those who refer you with even more attention so that they continue to refer you. Thank them for each referral, and continue to send them newsletters and correspondence to maintain the relationship.

Part 2: The Tools of Referral

There is an art to getting people to refer you, and it's not as simple as just keeping in contact with them.

You need to give them *easy ways to refer to you*. And this is done by using tools of referral.

A **book** is one of the **best tools of referral around**, so long as you leverage it wisely.

It's not enough to say, *"If you know anyone who needs an attorney for their [fill in the blank] case, have them call me."* That approach just isn't going to give you the outcome you want and need.

However, if you visit a bunch of body shops and pain doctors and bail bondsmen, and hand each of them 20 copies of your book to put in their lobby, then you've already done a lot in terms of stoking conversation and referrals. Leave them 50 or 100 business cards while you're at it.

This strategy has been used by past and present clients of Speakeasy Marketing, and it works. A bail bondsman can't directly recommend you to someone, but they can absolutely keep your books in their lobby, so that every person who walks through their doors can pick up a free copy.

And when that happens, your authority will suddenly be in the hands of potential clients *precisely when they need your authority the most.*

If you have not one but multiple books, as well as media and podcast or radio features, and logos and accolades peppering your website, then all of your referrals become more powerful.

That's because instead of your referral partners merely saying, *"Hey, you should talk to this attorney..."*

...They can say, *"Hey, this attorney has authored several books, they've been on the radio and podcasts, and they've even been on TV. They know what they're doing. And surprisingly, they offer pretty good prices."*

Don't you want to be the attorney who exudes so much authority and leaves such an impression on people, before they even meet them in person?

You want to create the perception that you charge a lot, because that is what attracts affluent clients. Affluent clients don't want the cheapest. They want the **best.** And if you follow the steps in this book, then they're going to see you and just *know* that's what they're getting.

Part 3: Consistency is the Key to Building Your Referral Network

This last part is simple: Consistently get your tools of referral into the right hands, and you'll see your referral network grow. This is how you expand your reach, generate tons of business, and enjoy a more lucrative practice than you ever thought possible.

We can help with all of this — every method, strategy, and tool discussed in this book.

Ready?

Call (888) 225-8594, email support@speakeasymarketinginc.com, or visit https://www.speakeasymarketinginc.com/.

As soon as you contact us, we'll have one of our authority experts get you on the road to enjoying **true, unmistakable authority in your field.**

It's waiting for you. You just have to go get it.

SECTION 3:

A BRUTALLY CANDID FIELD MANUAL TO ATTRACT AFFLUENT CLIENTS, AND BUILDING A FORMIDABLE LAW PRACTICE

 Tracy Merda
Senior Project Manager,
Speakeasy Marketing, Inc.
Jacobs & Whitehall Publishing

Dear Attorney,

Around here, we often talk about building a formidable law practice.

But what does that mean?

The 5 Hallmarks of a Formidable Law Practice

It means:

(1) One that inspires FEAR in the hearts of your competitors.

That makes them look at your website, your online presence, even your business card, and feel completely and utterly demoralized about competing with you directly.

(2) One that provokes a sense of AWE among your peers.

I'm talking about journalists, potential referral partners, and other people of influence within your community. That makes them say: "This gal is clearly the expert. What does SHE have to say?"

(3) One that commands the CONFIDENCE of affluent, high-quality clients.

That provides an immediate sense of reassurance that you are the one attorney who understands their needs, and not just some run-of-the-mill lawyer. (We'll talk about why this is important in a moment.)

(4) One that is RESILIANT to economic hardships.

Not because its bank account is stuffed full of cash (though, it may well be). And not because it enjoys a full pipeline of quality case leads. But because it serves the one segment of the US economy that,
historically, keeps getting richer and richer every year, even when everyone else gets poorer.

(5) Is UNRIVALED in the market.

That stands in a true category of one, and is unable to be directly compared with any "competing" firm or lawyer. Where you're the only one at the party, and can charge pretty much whatever you want.

This Kind of Practice Isn't for Every Attorney...

There's a price that has to be paid to create this kind of presence and positioning in your market. And, frankly, it's a price that many aren't willing to pay. However, if you are, over the coming pages, I'm going to share with you a foolproof strategy for making it happen. For making this the year you finally build the law practice you deserve. Over seven achievable milestones.

Before I do, though, we need to get clear about a few things.

You might even call these "threshold issues". Three specific questions that we need to examine carefully, and which you need to answer a clear, unequivocal YES to before we can proceed.

Threshold Issue #1:
Do you WANT to build a more formidable law practice?

A lot of attorneys don't.

They just want to leave the office an hour earlier, or free up some time for playing golf. Otherwise, their practice is perfectly fine, thank you very much. They don't want to fundamentally change its market positioning. Maybe you're the same. And there's nothing wrong with that.

However, if you do — if you want to attract a higher-caliber of client, have more of them calling you each week, and have strong enough positioning that you can command extraordinarily high fees (even if your metro area is swarming with cheaper juniors) — answer "aye" to this question now.

Then we can move to the next threshold issue. Which is about how to actually create this transformation. This is one that, in my experience, you're either going to buy into right away, or will recoil in disgust at what I'm about to suggest to you.

Threshold Issue #2:
Are you prepared to move to where the money is?

Consider the American economy a pyramid.

The base of the pyramid is made up of all the folks out there who, for whatever reason, are struggling to make ends meet. Folks who mostly live a hand-to-mouth existence. Or, to be blunt, have no money to hire a lawyer. Leave this world to the public defenders.

Above that, you have the middle of the pyramid. The middle classes. The folks who, when push comes to shove, can sell something, or take out a loan, or max out their credit card, or otherwise just about pull together enough cash to cover your fees. Provided you charge a reasonable "market rate". This is where most solos and small firms find their clients.

At the top, you have the affluent. This includes the mass affluent, high-net-worth individuals, ultra-high-net-worth individuals, and the Super Rich. These are the people who can afford — and are accustomed to getting — the best when it comes to almost everything. Clothes. Cars. Professional help. Almost every attorney wants to attract these people as clients. But very few do.

Here's something you already know:

The middle layer of that pyramid — the slice of the American economy where almost every solo attorney and law firm is competing for clients — it is rapidly disappearing. (The OECD defines "middle class" as those earning between 75% and 200% of the median income. The percentage of folks who fall into that bracket has shrunk by ~10% for each of the last four generations.)

In other words, this segment of the legal market is a shrinking pie.

Yet, since law school keeps pumping out more and more junior attorneys who don't have jobs to go to, every year sees more and more hungry hands fight it out for fewer and fewer clients who have less and less money to spend. You don't want to be a dog in this fight.

Now, here's the big reveal:

According to data from the Pew Research Center, the reason for the shrinking of the American middle class is NOT entirely that people are getting poorer every year. There's another factor: more folks are becoming affluent. In other words, the top section of the pyramid is growing.

These are the people who — when they wake up one morning and realize they need a lawyer — are more likely to come to you with a $100k, a $1MM, or sometimes even a $1MM+ legal problem. The people who need, expect, and can afford to hire the best attorney they can find.

This is the one segment of the market for legal services that has a rising tide. And it's also the one segment most attorneys struggle to attract. Ergo, if you're an attorney who is intent on building a formidable practice, then as "obvious" as it may sound when we put it this way...

Affluence Is Where the Money Is At

Hence, the second threshold issue for building a formidable practice:

Are you prepared to cede your seat at the "middle class" buffet to other attorneys, and position yourself as an attorney for affluent clients? If your answer is an "AYE", let's keep talking.

Because, throughout the rest of this guide, I'm going to reveal why most attorneys struggle to attract these clients. And how you can earn their attention and command their respect.

* * *

So, you want to attract affluent clients?

People who call with a $100k, $1MM, or even $10MM legal problem?

Able and willing to pay for expert, experienced counsel?

Over the following pages, we're going to talk about what it takes to show up on their radar, command their attention, and earn their respect. And, I'm going to reveal the reason...

Why Most Attorneys Fail Miserably to Attract These "Diamond-Grade" Clients

For there is a specific reason. In order to understand why it matters, it helps to examine how mass-market (i.e. middle-class) clients see attorneys differently to the way affluent clients do — how they come into your office or on Zoom with very different needs.

The middle class is, broadly speaking, a population of consumers.

When they need to find a lawyer, they literally shop online the same way they might shop around for a new laptop or automobile. They've been trained to search for value. They want the maximum number of "features" for the minimum price. And they are, for the most part, very price sensitive.

You've seen this.

These potentials come into your office, and they'll sit and listen for 30-45 minutes as you unpack their situation and try to explain the seriousness of their predicament and what they stand to lose if they try to cut compromise and hire a cheaper attorney who doesn't have your same depth of expertise and experience. It goes in one ear and out the other. And then they'll say something like:

"I spoke with another attorney this morning, and he said he can take on my case for only $2,000. Plus, he'll do three court appearances instead of just two. Can you match that? Otherwise...."

This is price-shopping behavior. From someone who has been conditioned to shop for "value".

Affluent clients are very different.
Generally speaking, the affluent are a population of investors. That is part of the reason why they are affluent. They have a different attitude to money. When they experience a legal problem, or realize they need the services of an attorney, they would never dream of shopping around online.

In fact, many of them detest shopping. Instead, they'll approach it the same way they approach most of the other of life's challenges that require professional help. They seek an advisor. But not just any advisor. They're looking for an expert advisor. An experienced and reputable professional who is considered the authority in their field or line of work.

This behavior extends to many different areas of life.

When their daughter starts having fits, they don't look for "a doctor". They seek out the leading neurologist in their state who specializes in adolescent epilepsy. And when they find him or her, price is almost never an issue. When their horse starts limping, they don't call the local veterinarian. They seek out the equine veterinarian who authored the book on laminitis. When their son develops an addiction for prescription drugs, they don't look for just "any" drug rehab center. They look for the center is considered the leading rehabilitator for white-collar prescription drug addicts. Likewise, when a large corporation approaches them about buying their family business, they don't look for a corporate attorney. They look for the expert who authored the book on M&A for SMB entrepreneurs.

Affluent clients aren't shopping around for "value".

What are they seeking?

Well… this brings us to the final threshold issue.

Threshold Issue #3:
Are you willing to elevate your positioning?

Affluent clients are attracted to AUTHORITY. Because it represents "safety" to them, in the same way that "saving money on legal fees" represents "safety" to middle-class consumers.

Frankly, they cannot afford to save money on their legal fees. There's simply too much at stake. Instead, they seek out the best their money can buy.

"Best", in this case, meaning "the authority on my situation". The reason most solo attorneys and small law firms fail to consistently attract these kinds of clients is, simply, that they are not seen as the authority. They are not perceived as "the" attorney for people like them.

An important note about this:

When it comes to attracting affluent clients, authority is not an "either-you-have-it-or-you-don't" phenomenon. It's a question of relative degree. **The higher up the economic pyramid you want to climb, the more relative authority you need, as compared with your peers, to attract them.**

If you want billionaires as clients, you need to be the most respected authority in your practice area or specialization in all of America. In some cases, the world. (Divorce tourism is a very real phenomenon.) If you "merely" want to attract the mass-affluent, it's enough to be the one attorney in your metro area who wrote the book on a particular legal problem (e.g. college students accused of sex crimes, doctors pulled over for DUI). For the affluent, high-net-worth, and

Super Rich, your level of perceived authority needs to be somewhere in between these two points.

And that's what the rest of this guide is about.

Over the following pages, I'm going to share with you seven specific steps you can follow to snowball your authority — seven milestones that take you from where you are right now to being THE respected authority for a particular type of affluent client.

Ready for the ride?

Authority Snowball Step #1: Your "Declaration of Authority"

If you're still reading this, then we agree on three things.

- **First**, that you want to build a more formidable law practice.

- **Second**, that the best way to do that — possibly the ONLY way — is to market your services to affluent potentials, rather than the mass market.

- And **third**, that affluence is attracted to authority.

Now that we have addressed these three "threshold issues", let's talk how you can actually build that authority. It's a seven-step journey that we call the Authority Snowball — and, over the space of about a year, it can take you from being perceived as "just another attorney on Avvo" to "the attorney". The one attorney who, for a certain type of client or legal problem, is considered the respected authority. The one attorney whose name and business card gets passed around at weddings and country clubs. The lawyer who affluence seeks out. It all starts with your Declaration of Authority.

This is the seed that will become your indomitable authority positioning. The clump of snow in your fist that will become an authority snowball. The first milestone in our seven-step journey to a formidable practice. And it's a fundamental, strategic statement that defines your positioning:

"I am THE attorney for people who _____."

A quick note, before we go any further with this. Authority positioning isn't something that has to define or constrain you. It's an asset. Something you own that works for you. Something you leverage.

What I mean by this is, when you come up with your own declaration of authority and then invest in transforming that declaration into bona fide positioning, it doesn't mean you stop taking on other cases.

In fact, a lot of our attorney authors own two or more authority positions, which they market as "satellite" websites to their main practice. We'll come back to this later. For now, I just want you to know that going through this process doesn't need to affect any of your other marketing or outreach.

It's a new, separate thing.

Now, this first step, figuring out the blank space above, this is one of the things we figure out during the first step of the Speak-a-Book process, which is the 30-minute strategy session. I do this every day, and I've developed a method for helping attorneys figure out what their "thing" is that they can transform into authority positioning and use to attract affluent clients.

For example, one of our authors is a criminal defense attorney. He is, now, also considered THE attorney for college students in Ann Arbor who have been wrongly accused of a sex crime. He literally wrote the book on that, and also followed some of the other steps I'm going to share.

Is this everything he does? No. Absolutely not. He takes on all kinds of other interesting cases. However, this authority positioning is an asset that brings him affluent clients.

You have something like this too. We just need to find it.

Maybe it's a particular kind of case that you really enjoy, or that is especially lucrative for you. Perhaps it's a certain type of client. Or, it might be a cause that resonates with you. It could even be all three.

Another one of our clients is considered THE attorney in Colorado for cyclists who have been injured on the road. For the right kind of clients, these cases can pay very well indeed. He also loves to help folks get what they deserve, so they can go and rebuild their lives. And – in some cases – his work even leads to policy change or remedial action that improves road safety for cyclists.

What about you? If you're serious about becoming a respected authority and building a more formidable practice, you need to figure out your Declaration of Authority.

All the other six steps build on this first one.

AUTHORITY SNOWBALL STEP #2: AUTHORING YOUR BOOK (THE EASY AND ETHICAL WAY)

This second step is about making your authority real, by creating a tangible "authority artefact".
Something you can physically give to clients. I'm talking, of course, about authoring a book.

When you're the author of a bona fide, officially published book, it instantly changes how you are perceived. It shifts your positioning, by letting potentials know that you are the real deal.

Because here's the thing:

Any attorney can brainstorm ideas over a glass of Scotch, and then come into the office the next morning and declare that they are an authority. In fact, it's exactly what a lot of professionals do. They hang their shingle as an authority on a certain type of problem, situation, or solution. Just as dozens of juniors hang their shingle as actual practicing lawyers the day after being admitted to the Bar.

Who are they kidding?

Declaring yourself an authority doesn't actually make you an authority any more than making the Bar makes you a real lawyer. Affluent potentials know this. They're not stupid. That's why they're affluent.

Authoring a book makes your authority real.

For the simple reason that, while any attorney can say they have a wealth of experience in a particular type of case or situation, it takes a real expert to author a book about it.

Take your favorite type of case, for example:

How many of your competitors claim it as their expertise too?

Probably dozens.

But how many wrote the book on it? None, most likely. And this is why authoring a book is the ante for any attorney who is serious about building a name as the authority for a certain type of case or legal situation — for any attorney who wants to attract affluent clients.

Frankly, if you don't want to author a book, you might as well go home. Because affluent clients won't take you seriously as an expert. I don't say this to be rude. But to really drive this vital point home.

If there's one step that, more than any other, radically transforms the way high-quality clients see you viz-a-viz your competitors, it's having a book. Because it gives you so much leverage.

It's a new title you can add to all your profiles and business cards.

It's an authority artifact you can mention in all of your marketing and communications with potential clients. (Don't be shy about this. Let them know that you are the author of a book on their situation, and that it's for sale in Barnes & Noble, on Amazon.com, and other popular platforms.) It's a physical gift you can hand to potentials, existing clients, referral partners, local journalists, even organizers, non-profits, etc. It's a fantastic referral tool. (It's easier for someone to tell their friend or client to "request a complimentary book online" than to "call a lawyer").

You have to remember:

Almost all of your peers, competitors — they too have a JD, they too are Board-Certified, and they too probably have a 10.0 Avvo rating. Consequently, these things give you zero competitive advantage.

Sorry. But if this is all you bring to the table in terms of authority, there's NOTHING to differentiate you from cheaper competitors. That's how affluent clients see things. You will literally be invisible to them. You won't exist. Authoring a solid book, though... It immediately puts you in a category of one.

So, step two of the Authority Snowball method, after you've figured out your Declaration of Authority, is to waste no time in transforming it into a book. You need to make your authority real.

I can help you nail both of these steps together, in one fell swoop. Apply to the Speak-a-Book program today. It takes only a few minutes, and, at this point, no payment info is required. After we review your application, you'll get a call back from my colleague Dennis, who is the Director of Author Admissions. He will be able to talk through the specifics of the program, answer any questions, etc. Then you and I will jump on the phone. We'll figure out your Declaration of Authority, and then get the ball rolling on transforming it into a professional-looking, officially published book. And with just 2-3 hours of work required from you. When February rolls on by, you could already be well on your way to building your authority snowball and creating the formidable practice you deserve.

AUTHORITY SNOWBALL STEP #3: WHAT IF YOU'RE NOT THE FIRST AUTHOR IN YOUR LEGAL NICHE?

The legal profession has become more and more competitive every year. In many specific metro/practice areas, there are dozens of attorneys all fighting to position themselves as the pre-eminent authority. And one or two have even published a book. How are you to compete with that?

The answer can be found by looking into other industries.

Specifically, the self-help industry.

Go walk around the self-help section of your local Barnes & Noble and you'll see many hundreds of different titles from just as many self-professed gurus, on topics from finance to health, weight loss to dating, careers to spirituality. It's a very, very crowded space. Yet, there are a few names at the top that have successfully dominated this ruthlessly competitive industry for more than a decade, and they are still going strong. Try as they might, the upstarts can't knock them off their pedestals.

Why? Because they took their original book, and turned it into a franchise.

You might or might not know who Mark Victor Hansen is. Or Robert Kiyosaki. Or Robert Greene. However, I assure you, they are titans in their field. People pay thousands of dollars to stand up for hours and listen to them rattle off some variation of the same speech you can listen to for free on YouTube. They'll wait in line for hours for the opportunity to have a selfie next to them. Even when there are thousands of other experts who are smarter, more interesting, and who will literally PAY MONEY to get up on the same stage and speak. What's their secret?

Mark Victor Hansen is the "Chicken Soup for the Soul" guy. He didn't just write a book. He authored, co-authored, and repurposed many dozens of spin-off "Chicken Soup for the Soul" books, and he owns that brand. A brand that is, by many estimates, worth more than $10 million.

Robert Kiyosaki is the "Rich Dad, Poor Dad" guy. He didn't just write one good book. He turned it into several derivative works. It's now his brand. A brand that has allowed him to amass a fortune.

Robert Greene?

You know who Greene is. The "X Laws of Insert-Nefarious-Endeavor-Here" guy. He parlayed a cult classic, *The 48 Laws of Power*, into a franchise. He "co-authored" another book with 50 Cent.

Now, you're no self-help guru.

But you can use a modified version of this same strategy to position yourself as an authority figure who is a level or two above the "mere author". And there's a clever shortcut.

A method that allows you to achieve this feat in as little as 45 days, and without having to author multiple different books from scratch. What is it? **Speak-a-Book Platinum**.

An optional upgrade to our regular Speak-a-Book service, where we conduct a second content interview (around 45-60 minutes in length) after your book is finished. We then use the resulting content to create two ADDITIONAL book titles, where your first book is adapted for two niches.

Each of the two spin-off books is 90% the same content, plus one new chapter, a unique introduction, and several other unique elements to justify its being a different title.

By the way, this is exactly what Mark Victor Hansen did with his Chicken Soup for the Soul spin-offs. They're mostly repurposed material, just repackaged for multiple difference niche markets.

How Might an Attorney Turn His or Her Authority Book into a Franchise?

Take one of our recent Speak-a-Book of the Months, for example.

Defeating Your Reckless Driving Ticket in Virginia, by Attorney Michael C. Huff.

If Mr. Huff wanted to, he could jump on the phone for another "content extraction" interview, which would take about an hour. We would then use the content to create two variant books that are 90% the same book, but have a unique introduction, one unique chapter, a unique author biography section, and, of course, unique front and back covers. For two specific niches.

For example, *Defeating Your Reckless Driving Ticket in Virginia for Healthcare Workers* and *Defeating Your Reckless Driving Ticket in Virginia for Business Owners.* Both separate, officially published titles.

Ideally, Mr. Huff would do this for two of his most lucrative niches, or for a new niche that he wants to dominate. And next time a potential from one of these niches contacts his firm, he can send them a book about their unique situation. Which would make his positioning UNASSAILABLE.

More importantly, when an affluent client visits his website, he or she will see that he isn't a "mere author", but is the author of a franchise of books. And all he had to invest, timewise, was an additional 60 minutes or so, beyond the standard Speak-a-Book process, to get THREE books.

Does this sound like something you should do? If so, apply to the Speak-a-Book program today, and when you get on the phone with Dennis, ask him about this upgrade.

Again, it's called **Speak-a-Book Platinum**.

AUTHORITY SNOWBALL STEP #4: WHEN (AFFLUENT) POTENTIALS "SIZE YOU UP" ONLINE

At this point — if you were to implement the previous three steps — you have laid claim to a position as the authority for a certain type of client or case, you have authored a book to make that authority positioning real, and you have parlayed your book into a series or franchise of related books.

What next?

It's time to leverage your book into an online multimedia authority platform, so that, when affluent potentials size you up online, their jaw is on the floor.

Let me unpack that a little.

As you know, people absolutely DO size you up online.

Any time your name is passed around, or someone hears about you on the news, or receives your newsletter, or stumbles upon your ad or profile in a directory, the first thing they do is visit your website or Google your name. What they see immediately defines where they place you.

If your presence looks like that of your peers, you will be put in their category. A list of about a dozen names with yours at the bottom. Options for them to consider. Vendors.

You don't want to be an option or a vendor. You want to immediately position yourself as THE respected authority on their particular situation, so they see and relate to you as a trusted advisor.

One way to do that:

Transform your website into the digital version of what we, as direct marketers, might call a "shock and awe package". A collection of high-quality, deep content, credibility markers, and other authority assets that immediately communicate your stature. (By the way, this is something almost all financial advisors, investment professionals, and other trusted advisors who market their services to affluent people or families have working for them. It's the *sine non qua* for this game.)

Ideally, you need to have:

- A library of written content articles — not "fluff" (i.e. keyword-stuffed) content, but deep content that mirrors the kind of language affluent potentials use, answers their most common questions, and also provides useful insights to them while telling your story

- A collection of videos — this can be the same content as the articles, presented as either "talking head" videos or as presentation slides

- A series of podcast episodes — where each episode is short and sweet, and focused on a particular point or question from your book

- Ads for requesting a complimentary or paid copy of your book — shown on the homepage, at the end of every content piece, and on sidebars.

- Logos for Amazon.com, Barnes & Noble, Audible, Kindle, and any other platforms where your book is listed for sale.

- Badges for recognized podcast platforms, including the Apple Podcasts app, Google

Podcasts app, Spotify, iHeart Radio, Overcast, etc.

- Physical photographs of you holding your book.

Now, here's the thing:

You Don't Actually Need to Create ANY New Content from Scratch...

And that's because our program provides you, after your book is published, with an MS Word document that contains all your book's content serialized into ~12-15 separate content articles. You, your admin assistant, or your "web guy" can literally copy and paste them into WordPress and publish them as blogs or articles.

And, if you want the videos and podcasts too?

We offer another optional upgrade for the Speak-a-Book program called Authority Platform — where, again, after your book has been published, we use its content to create and fill out a "turn-key" website that contains all of the elements I just listed above, i.e. the written blogs/articles, video library, podcast series, ads and lead-gen forms for your book, logos, badges, etc.

We take care of everything.

And we set it up as a second "satellite" website that is 100% independent from your practice's main website, and has no effect on its SEO rankings. What's more, we also set up various different channels (e.g. Vimeo, Apple Podcasts, Google Podcasts, etc.) and syndicate all your content out.

And we publish your book on Audible as an audiobook.

It's a 12-month program. So, if you were to get started now — by the time this month rolls around next year, you'll have the ultimate online authority platform. The ultimate "digital shock and awe package". Ready for when folks size you up.

Interested in learning more? Ask Dennis about the Authority Platform upgrade (available to new and existing Speak-a-Book authors) when you jump on the phone with him as part of the application process.

AUTHORITY SNOWBALL STEP #5: GETTING FEATURED/QUOTED IN THE MEDIA

"Are you nuts?"

Thus asked an attorney-at-law who reads this newsletter.

He continues: "I already have more clients and cases than I can possibly handle, I am subbing work out to other attorneys, and doing pro bono cases because I feel guilty about how much money I am earning. I do NOT need or want more cases. . . give me a break. . ."

Good for him. And if you're in this position as well, good for you.

However, most attorneys who I speak with on the phone almost every day aren't so fortunate. Their phones aren't ringing. Or they're not ringing enough. Or, if they are ringing, the people at the other end of the line are not the affluent, high-quality potentials they need to feed a thriving law practice. These attorneys do need a break. In fact, what they really need is a kick-start. Some new ideas and strategies they can use to transform their firms throughout the year ahead — methods that are not immediately obvious, that are proven to work, that our most successful clients are using to attract "cream-of-the-crop" cases. And that's why I created this guide, to provide some new ideas.

We've talked about step one of the Authority Snowball, which is about defining your niche of affluent clients. Then we looked at step two, which was where you position yourself as the authority for this niche — by authoring the book on whichever specific type of case, situation, need, legal problem, or client you want to specialize in. Step three was about transforming your authority book into a series of books, so you own a franchise. And then, in the previous section, we looked at step four:

This is where you leverage your book — and its official presence on Amazon.com, Barnes & Noble, Kindle, and other platforms, as well as all its content — to create an online "shock and awe" platform that leaves potentials sitting there with an open mouth when they go to size you up online.

We're now on to step five, which is about using your book, and all the other authority assets you've parlayed from it, to get featured and quoted in the local media.

There are two reasons you want to do this:

First, because it gets you noticed. People see you in the newspaper, hear you on the radio, and watch you on TV. They spot you over the internet. And they see you as a pre-eminent public figure.

Your stature is increased.

Second, because it attracts quality leads. When someone reads a piece you wrote or a piece that quotes you, and they like what they hear, they are going to look you up online. Especially if they need a lawyer.

But these two things are just perks.

They're not the REAL reason you want to get in the media. The real reason is that being featured and quoted in the media gives you additional authority assets — a plethora of them — that, in terms of credibility, count for more than anything you could ever write or say about yourself.

So, how do you do it?

There Are Really <u>Three Secrets</u> to Getting Your or Your Firm's Name in the Media

Secret #1:

Make yourself more than "just an attorney". Put yourself forward as an attorney, as the author of a book (or, better, a series of books), and as the champion of a cause that has considerable public interest.

Journalists are constantly pestered by lawyers and other local business owners who want free publicity. What they really want is a hero. Someone who is the "voice" of an issue. Be that voice.

Secret #2:

Make a stellar introduction. Shock and awe. Don't just send a letter or a press release. Send a complimentary copy of your book, along with a letter of introduction and media one sheet that lays out all your authority assets and puts your absolute best foot forward.

Dozens of your competitors send press releases. I'd bet that NONE of them are published authors, and send out a complimentary copy of their book. That puts you in a category of one.

Secret #3:

Don't just be persistent. Be relentless.

Even if you don't hear back from your "shock-and-awe" letter of introduction, keep every editor, journalist, and other media contact on a "hot" list and send them a physical copy of your newsletter every month. Or, send them a cutting or recording every time you're featured or mentioned.

The idea is this:

As some point, the said editor, journalist, or media contact is going to run a piece about a topic that is closely related to your chosen legal niche. And you want them to immediately think of you.

For example, earlier I told you about one of our attorney authors who published a book on road safety and cycling in Colorado. When, God forbid, a cyclist is injured or killed on the road and there's outrage, who do you think they'll call for a quote? The attorney who champions this cause.

A friend of mine calls this the "Armrest Strategy". When he flies on an airplane and he's not fast enough to get dibs on both armrests, he uses a variation of this same method to "wrest" it from the passengers next to him. What he'll do is keep his elbow close to his sides and watch that armrest like a hawk, never forgetting about it or giving up. When his unfortunate neighbor lifts their hand to scratch their nose or take their coffee from the hostess, he'll quickly slide it onto the armrest. He doesn't know when it will happen. Sometimes he waits only a few minutes. Sometimes an hour or longer. But he persistently plays the game. It's an ingrained habit. This is how you get in the news.

Position yourself as an authority. Champion some kind of cause or position. And keep sending things to every contact on your media list relentlessly, until they need someone like you for a quote.

Also, please, please, please:

Create a new page on your practice's main website and/or your secondary "authority platform" website, and detail all the media mentions you get. Put logos and names of publications all over your website.

If you don't blow your own trumpet, there's no music.

Apply for the Speak-a-Book program right now. You'll get a media one-sheet, letter of introduction, and six months of newsletters to send out.

Everything you need to execute the strategy above.

All created using content from your Speak-a-Book. So, no work from you required. You can literally hand these to your admin to send out.

AUTHORITY SNOWBALL STEP #6: THE JOE ROGAN EXPERIENCE (FOR LAWYERS)

A few years ago, most folks had never heard of Joe Rogan. Those who had knew him as one of the commentators for the Ultimate Fighting Championship, or as a B- or C-list actor and comedian.

Now? He's one of the hottest and most influential names in showbiz.

Actors, billionaires, A-list celebrities, and even the occasional quantum physicist fall over themselves to appear as a guest on his show for free. Which, by the way, is not even a "real" TV show. It's a podcast. *The Joe Rogan Experience*. It's one of the hottest podcasts going at the moment. And, over the last few years, it has even become a "crown jewel" that gurus, thought leaders, and rising celebrities want in their hands — to show that they are a somebody.

Why?

Because Joe Rogan has amassed an audience. An audience of podcast listeners who lead lives, experience things, and spend money. Listeners who are influenced by the ideas and people Rogan brings to them. And, when they appear on his podcast, they immediately get to leverage his credibility.

My point is this:

A few years ago, podcasts were something the kids did. Not anymore. They're mainstream now.

And if you're an attorney who is serious about positioning himself or herself as an authority figure — especially, as an authority figure for affluent clients who are looking for the best their money can buy — then you need to start showing up on podcasts too, lest people think you're a nobody.

There are podcasts for almost everything.
A lot of them are garbage.

But many of them have become valuable online and offline real estate. Especially those that are targeted to the affluent and high-net-worth. Appearing on them is a great way to attract new potentials.

However, as we saw yesterday, the real value is in how it elevates your positioning. Because, when you appear as an expert guest on another guru's podcast — even if it is someone most folks have never heard of — you now have an extremely valuable authority asset to show off on your website.

You can upload an audio or video recording.

You can link to the original podcast.

You can display a "behind-the-scenes" photograph somewhere. (Notice that almost all of Joe Rogan's celebrity guests do this? Because it works.)

You can mention it in all your letters and profiles.

You can drop it into casual conversation.

Now, getting invited on to high-value podcasts — where other A-list experts and respected authority figures are featured — it's a lot like being invited to glamorous parties. If you're an accepted part of the "scene", it just happens without you needing to do anything. You receive invitations. Your name is passed around. But if you're not, it can be difficult to break in.

Nonetheless, some of our authors have succeeded.

Here are two insider secrets that will help:

First, the people you need to approach are not the podcast hosts themselves. At the level you want to play, these hosts have handlers. You can't reach them. It's the podcast producers you need to contact. They are the folks on whose radar you need to show up. They are the ones who select guests.

Follow the method I shared for the previous step, which was step five, to cultivate a list of podcast producers who have you in their Rolodex as an authority on an area of law that is of interest to their audience. Use your book and other authority assets to establish strong positioning. Because the last thing you want to appear as is "just another lawyer".

And the second insider secret?

Getting that first professional podcast experience is the toughest.

Because you're a new face, a new voice, a new name.

Nobody really knows what you bring to the table.

However, once you have that first podcast under your belt — a real podcast, that is professionally produced — everything becomes a lot easier. You now have a "demo" you can pass to producers.

We're about to launch a new legal podcast. It's called *The Legal Thought Leaders Podcast*. And it's a platform for featuring and promoting experienced attorneys who are working on the cutting edge of their practice areas — who represent the pinnacle of excellence in their niche or practice area.

Appearance is strictly by invitation only. (There will also be a fee.) However, we're giving careful consideration and priority to Jacobs & Whitehall authors, for the simple reason that they "wrote the book" on what they do. I'll tell you more about this podcast over the coming weeks and months.

As well as getting exposure and publicity to an audience of affluent people who, for their own reasons, have an interest in listening to and learning from some of America's sharpest and most experience lawyers — our guests will benefit from a complimentary recording of their podcast episode, which they can use to command the respect of other podcast hosts and land more appearances.

(We will also provide references and letters of introduction.)

One more perk of being a Speak-a-Book author.

Ready to get started on a book? Ready to invest in an authority asset that you can snowball into niche dominance? If so, I'm ready to jump on the phone with you and get started.

Authority Snowball Step #7: Building a Dependable Referral Machine

Now, we reach the seventh and final step of the Authority Snowball.

This is where we leverage all authority assets that you've created and laid down so far — the book (or series of books), the online multimedia authority platform, the media features, your podcast features — and use them to build out a network of referral partners from different professions.

The key word here is "build". We're not going to wait around passively and hope that somebody will send one of their clients to you. We're going to proactively build a stream.

How? By working with human psychology. Rather than against it.

As you know, referral leads are the crème de la crème. Even more so with affluent clients. They come to you pre-sold, and often pre-qualified, on retaining you. And they are usually better-behaved clients as well. Even when you need to pay a 10%+ referral fee to other attorneys, the money is still 100% worth it. For all of the time and hassle you save.

Here's the thing, though:

While it is immensely valuable, this stream of quality leads is really the secondary benefit of building a referral network. The primary benefit is the added authority you get. When your name keeps getting passed around and dropped, and potentials hear good things about you from multiple different sources, it now MULTIPLIES the power of everything else we've seen.

Almost every attorney wants a solid referral network.

Many attempt to build one.

Most fail. For three main reasons:

First, they restrict their outreach to other attorneys. What's more, they often restrict themselves to attorneys who are not directly "competing" for clients. This is a mistake.

While it's true that only other attorneys can get paid to refer cases to you, it doesn't mean other professionals are not motivated to refer to you as well. Many are. Especially when you are the respected authority who literally authored the book on the very problem their clients face.

You need to think outside the box. What other professional advisors do your ideal clients work with? Who else do they turn to for advice and guidance? Who else do they respect?

Are they likely to approach or retain another kind of attorney before they realize they need your expertise? Do you have competitors who actively market to the same clients, who, like you, are sometimes too busy? Who would rather refer a client to a "competitor" than earn nothing?

Where do your ideal clients socialize? Who do they confide in?

All of these people need to be added to a list of potential referral partners. These are the people with whom you need to cultivate a relationship. Which brings us to the next mistake most attorneys make:

They ask only once.

You need to keep showing up in front of these potential referral partners. They need to keep seeing your name, and they need to keep seeing quality content from you that gives them a flavor of the kind of expertise you offer. **Ideally, you should be sending something once every month.**

Remember when we talked about sending a cover letter, one sheet, and monthly newsletters to your media contacts? As well as clippings and links to media features and podcasts, as you accumulate them? Well, send the same material to your list of potential referral partners as well.

And the third mistake?

You need to lower the bar. Make it as easy as humanly possible for partners to refer their potentials or clients to you. And make it as easy and non-threatening as possible for these referred leads to raise their hand and ask for more information from you.

This is (yet) another area where having a book helps. It's much, MUCH easier to get someone to request a complimentary book than it is to get them to pick up the phone to talk with a lawyer. It's simply a smaller step. Make this your referral mechanism. When you reach out to referral partners in your first communication, tell them about your book. Tell them how it retails in Barnes & Noble. Tell them how you would be happy to send a complimentary copy out in the mail to any name they send your way, and with *their* compliments. And keep telling them in every follow-up.

Now, just because this is the seventh step of the Authority Snowball method, it doesn't mean you need to wait to implement it. It's a process you can kick-start right away, as soon as your new book is done.

FINAL THOUGHTS: START OF A NEW ERA?

As I write this, we stand on the threshold of an important moment.

Joe Biden, of course, is about to be inaugurated as the 46th President of the United States. And it feels like our democracy, our society, even our very way of life stands upon the edge of a knife, to paraphrase Tolkien. If Biden strays but a little, it might all fail to the ruin of us all.

Yet, hope remains.

Now, I bear no ill will toward our new President. I wish him the very best of luck, and pray that his presidency is the start of an era of healing. God knows we all need it right now.

But, me, personally — I refuse to place all my hope in politicians.
If anyone is going to lift America out of this abyss, it's us. The people who keep our world going round. The professionals like you who serve on the front line of society. It's we who must now step up.

America was built on ambition.

On the relentless struggle for greatness and success.

It's what being American is about.

And, in my humble opinion, the way for us to heal America and get our great nation back on its feet is to be Americans — to get out of bed every morning with an unquenchable fire of ambition raging in our hearts, ready to build. Not destroy. Not tear down. BUILD.

Politicians are not our salvation.

Celebrities, media, and Big Tech are not our salvation.

WE must be our salvation.

What America desperately needs right now is for us all to get back to work, whatever way we can, given the COVID-19 pandemic. For us to build our businesses and create a rising tide of prosperity and hope.

Make this the best year you've ever had. And, IMHO, it's the most patriotic thing we can all do right now. America doesn't need more screaming protestors. It doesn't need more people standing outside public buildings with guns, beating public servants with flagpoles. And it certainly doesn't need more grandstanding. **It needs more Americans. Like you, and like me**.

Over the previous pages, I've laid out a seven-step strategy for dominating your chosen legal niche, by taking a fistful of snow, an intention, and turning it into an Authority Snowball. One day at a time.

If you're ready to kick-start this process by authoring a book, I'm ready to jump on the phone with you and help make it happen. Already, we have had dozens of attorneys apply to the Speak-a-Book Program and sign on as new authors. There's still space to work with you too.

I've asked our tech team to remove the limit of 15 attorneys. If I need to work late into the night for a few months to help you author your new book, so be it.

I'm ready for the challenge.

Are you?

Apply to the Speak-a-Book program now.

Authority is an incredible thing. It's also a precious thing. And, I believe, one of the reasons it is so powerful, so persuasive, is that it's sorely missing from our public life today. Folks crave bona fide authority. Especially legal clients. They are crying out for someone like you who can step into the fray and lead them to a place of safety. An attorney who, within their sphere, has seen and done almost everything. An attorney who can provide legitimate hope. But they're skeptical.

The world is full of people who are "all hat, no cattle" as we say here in Texas. People who pretend to be something or someone they're not. It takes authority to break through the skepticism.

Especially with affluent clients. But when you do, your positioning within your legal niche, even your entire metro/practice area, it can be transformed utterly. And your fortunes with it.

One of the wonderful things about authority: When you start showing up in multiple different places, you become omnipresent. And people start to wonder what all the fuss is about. Social proof.

I heard of a guy once who was a complete nobody. One day, as an experiment, he paid a mob of photographers to follow him around taking shots, as if they were the paparazzi. When he walked into clubs, people assumed he was a famous celebrity. And he was treated accordingly.

That's the power of all these authority assets. They build on each other, they multiply each other's power, and they compound. That's why we call this method the Authority Snowball.

If it can turn a "nobody" into a celebrity, imagine what it can do for you. Imagine how much your practice, and your life, could be completely and utterly transformed over the year ahead — when you get a book done and published, when you author a series of books, when you have one or more online authority platforms working for you, when you start showing up in all kinds of different offline media, when you appear on respected podcasts.

This kind of transformation could herald a new era of prosperity. For you and your family. For your staff, contractors, vendors who support you. For your community. For all the local businesses you patronize, who, now more than ever, desperately need your support as a customer. And for your country.

Our country.

Will you join me? Are you ready to be a part of the medicine American needs?

If so, I look forward to jumping on the phone with you soon.

NOTES